TEA AND SUBTITLES

TEA AND SUBTITLES

SELECTED POEMS
1999-2019

MICHAEL MILLER

MOON
TIDE PRESS

~2019~

Tea and Subtitles: Selected Poems 1999-2019
© Copyright 2019 Michael Miller

Editor-in-Chief
Eric Morago

Marketing Director
Dania Alkhouli

Marketing Assistant
Ellen Webre

Proofreader
Nancy Lynée Woo

Front cover art
Chris Miller

Author photo
Rachanee Srisavasdi

Book design
Michael Wada

Moon Tide logo design
Abraham Gomez

Tea and Subtitles: Selected Poems 1999-2019
is published by Moon Tide Press

Moon Tide Press #166
6745 Washington Ave. Whittier, CA 90601
www.moontidepress.com

FIRST EDITION

Printed in the United States of America

ISBN # 978-1-733949-3-3-0

Contents

III.

IV.

V.

Foreword

Michael Miller is a poet of generosity and expansiveness who invites us into a world of regular people and ordinary experiences and then reminds us how extraordinary life is, in all its variations. Writers are often thought of as observers, standing apart from the rest of humanity and taking notes, and Miller is certainly a keen observer. The empathetic nature of his vision, however, engages and includes writer, reader, and subject. Not standing apart but instead creating a sense of full immersion and immediacy, Miller helps us to see the value of particular human beings whose names we will never see in lights: a window washer, a street singer, a student learning English, a pool coach, an old bluesman. In "What We're Sure Of," the speaker in the poem tells how, on a rainy day, he "watched a woman huddle with her cart at the bus stop / while a plastic bucket gathered drops beside her. Each cupful / will have its use, laundry or wipes or a boiling mug of tea, / a source to ration…" He concludes, "our luck determines what we learn from rain."

These poems ask us to consider our own lives and the lives of those around us, including the combination of intimacy and strangeness in that gathering of houses we call a neighborhood. How should we behave towards those we live near but don't know well? Within our own homes, how do we make a family, and how do we continue to love one another in the face of instability or betrayal? Growing up, we struggle to understand this world we've been born into. At the moment of birth, a baby experiences "the only light that will rush in / without the memory of light before." At "Four and a Half," a shell is a "small blessing delivered / like a flake of sky." In "Ride Home," a child is learning how to keep secrets, "the art of leaving the right parts unsaid."

Artists and musicians are often our guides in these pages, as they struggle not only to understand but to translate the world into art, encountering life without the protective layers most develop to survive. To draw or play music, or, for that matter, to write poetry, is to ask the big questions through the particular ones, and the reward for being open to the pain of the world is to more deeply experience its beauty as well. As Miller writes in "Moment," "The girl with the sketchpad / is the lucky one here."

I am moved by so many of these poems because they acknowledge death and loss and grief while encouraging us to claim those moments of grace that keep us going. In "To Rachanee, Laguna Beach, Jan. 1," the speaker says, "let's enjoy / what is never given to us for keeps: / heaven, the absolute, whatever we name it." We may never understand death, despite the platitudes we come up with to deal with it, and we don't know exactly what heaven would be, but, as Miller writes in "One Word," "today offers its own grace."

Miller's poems have the authenticity of experience but never succumb to cynicism. In "Our Money's Worth," a couple is selling their old Honda and the speaker explains that "In our thirties now, / we have logged enough milestones / to know not to dwell on new ones." It's the moments of connection that matter, with family, with friends, with the mix of people you might encounter at a "Housewarming, East Los Angeles": "this touch of sky / and nearness with friends what we run to at any hour / when a room is not enough."

This sense of chosen community, and specifically poetic community, is beautifully evoked in "Ofrenda for John Gardiner," one of the last poems in the book. An "ofrenda" is an offering, a collection of objects for a person who has died, associated with *Día de los Muertos* celebrations. Elegizing Gardiner, a poet, Miller addresses him: "Dear clown, / teacher, jester who sweetened so much anger…" He tells his departed friend how his admirers and friends "shouldered your words / because they can only rest on shoulders now" and walked toward "where wonder begins."

This book, too, is a place where wonder begins. In clear language and with a poetic craft that carries us surely and cleanly through each poem, Michael Miller gives us ways of seeing that increase our sense of what it means to be alive in the world today, poems that point toward "true heaven / a light beyond our corneas, a truth beyond / the words we inscribe."

Jennifer Horne
Alabama Poet Laureate

For

Rachanee

and

Clare

I

Newborn

It starts with an illumination
the brightest there will ever be

the darkness pierced at the end of the bubble
and the sudden holocaust of white

the dreams welled up and carried surging
into slap of air and quaking breath

this box of four walls and a ceiling
bounding the new outrageous world

of hands that pass to larger hands
and colors teeming in every corner

the only light that will rush in
without the memory of light before

the cord cut and then the moment's lift
before the glide into expectant arms

the first taste of effortless flight
and the first fleeting touch down.

College Town

In a city awake on tea and subtitles,
the freshman boys fight off sleep
to hear a bluesman sing at the corner club,
his foot tapping and hoarse voice wailing

about fleeing the river hounds; and all the faces
look warm and dry here, the Lost Boys of Sudan
sheltered behind glass and glowing
on the art-house cinema, the neon sign

of the conquistador blinking over the nightclub
with his rifle drawn (the children of the Aztecs
on the sidewalk below seeking wristbands cool
in their pressed silk collars) — here the bus shakes

to a stop every hour, the doors snapping open
and the couples pass (consummated)
through ocean breeze and the crash of the fountain
in search of a drink — the girls in mascara

who glint like fireflies in the yellow lamps,
the one who breaks from the line at the tavern
and ducks into the gallery, past
the corner magician and the swirling eyes

of new babies, stands wet by the glare
of the bootleggers brutal and handsome under
their shaded brims in a portrait
in the hall, the newspapers cheering New Deal

and the trays of Cabernet in back (a finger
polished red half sober texting
about *free food, gallery show, what time
do u get off wk*) — the kisses stolen

over floodlights and the donation box
overflowing by ten, the eyes of migrants
that lust from photographs, the cards telling stories
of when this town was dust, when everyone was hungry.

The Chicago Window Washer Lets His Soap
Paintings Stay

If the cable snaps today,
              his ideas will not go with him.

     This time, he lets the hasty marks dry,
the lines usually swallowed
    by his wavering bucket of water
            now directing the sun's traffic through.

     With his rosary from Mexico in pocket
and Wacker Street below
        gray and sterile as a slab before surgery,

   he fastens his cable each dawn
          and scales the building's silent face.
Invisibility is the gift

     he gives the city,
   his fingers without documents
to be fingers for real

   dragging the blade's bent rubber
       until no trace stays behind.

     On the free days at the museum,
attended always in his one clean tie,

his eyes check the death dates beside the frames,
        the record of so many cords giving way.

When any body lands,
        what survives the blow at the bottom?

    He imagines the flight that follows,
        the dashing of breath and size and debt
            and the sky poised to catch the ideas and name.

        It is the fear of loud voices
    that keeps so much confined,
            so today, he has drawn
                where the yelling boss won't see.

    Before the office with the door shut all summer
and the mouse dangling where the modem sat,
            his Rothko
                cuts the sky in three:

        one layer splotchy,
        one streaked straight
            and pure light
                sandwiched in the middle.

    On half of the corner office
    that the recession voided,
three smashed Picasso men mark his sides.

        The trumpeter slouches, the rim of his hat
    tipped just enough to count the watching eyes.
        The rhythm player weeps, his bass a chronic load.

The singer leans back, nothing to be but happy.
The intersection will always cheer.
                The smile left after death

        is the only one
            not facing death down.

Poems at the Station

---

there is time and hopefully
a train
          —Lee Mallory

6:57 a.m.

Outline of a white oak stretched
on the sidewalk by the depot —
this shadow stayed as the frontier
gave to concrete below it.

10:30 a.m.

Bony child on the cup
and two dollars clang in.
The world is broken
and fixed every instant.

1:18 p.m.

Overtime and the state team
sets at the 10-yard line.
Time called. A tear shed?
Even police crowd the TV.

4:03 p.m.

Feet move around
the unscratched lottery ticket.
Behind them the toddler
stomps twice on every crack.

7:15 p.m.

Composer's face on magazines
and three headsets play the concerto.
Every great thought
like a syringe into the universe.

11:59 p.m.

Obituary shows on
the front page through the dispenser.
One fewer set of ears
will recognize the whistle.

The Beatles at 80

The public still demands them.
Every four years, as if by rote,
it reelects them to the city council,
their names never on the ballot
but each one too dutiful with age
to turn down another invitation.
The city clerk lines them up side-by-side
on the dais,
the matching jackets still vivid in her mind,
polishes their name plates every Tuesday

and pours four identical cups of tea.
They file in, slowly, and the audience stands.
The men remove their hats
while the gray-haired women clutch flowers
(the city never runs out of flowers)
and their sons and daughters clasp hands dutifully,
their iPods filled with countless other bands
but knowing the stories about sexual awakenings
and the 45s hoarded in council flats.
It has been decades

since the last guitar was packed away,
longer still since the last recording session.
But they know the eyes still watch them
and the media still hungers for quotes —
every few years bringing a new biography

or revisionist take on their sixties and seventies —
and they do their best to use their power for good:
Yes, the charter schools need endowments.
No, plastic is bad for the wetlands.
Yes, we're in favor of same-sex marriage;
we've always believed in peace and love.
Each one lives now

in his private compound,
their socializing limited to photo shoots
and meetings that drag until 1 a.m.
Every wardrobe change is a fashion statement,
every vacation to the East a pilgrimage.
When one falls ill or misses a vote,
the city braces itself again.
The bloggers tiptoe around the word *breakup.*
The editors finger the front-page layouts,
the ones headlined *END OF AN ERA*,
that they've held in check for half a century.
The crowd always, always, just has to look.

Woman Next Door

The door yanked open first and left
like an overture that builds to her voice,

she appears with one foot out of the house,
the Fender bass resisting the dig of her fingertips

before she stalks out and heaves it onto the lawn,
turns to flip the bird and storms back in.

In a second, she's out again — her retreats and exits
as abrupt as a boxer's steady left, right, left.

Her flight takes her to the street corner lamp,
the crossroads where she pauses, red and pierced,

each direction gleaming with its late-day overture
of turn signals, vacancy signs. From here,

behind the window glass, what can we do?
There has been no crime, no blood, no struggle,

no name or shared history that would beseech us
to tell off the man, clear the guest room for her.

Our hospitality quails at the conditions we've set.
All we have left is our own inspection: our eyes

that drift to the living room and mark the corners
without guitars or amps, the books we've checked out

for each other, the hour's small talk priming the air.
Each morning, each morning, we wake unaware

of the things we've won without trying.

Host

Before he passes the reefers out,
he checks himself in the mirror —
black jacket with the collar pressed,
hair parted,
skin like sand.
When he tore the cuff link on his right,
he lit her cigarette with his left —
knowing that when the hour was late,
she would never let herself be drugged
by a less than perfect hand.

Soprano

The soprano who sings
on this record player
and makes the hour seem twice as slow
passed away a long time ago
and doesn't remember recording this song.

They said she was hungry, slept too little,
wandered lonely by the docks at night.
The man from the chapel spreads out his bride
on the covers,
laughs as his palms give chase.

She laughs with him, maneuvers his fingers
down her chest, hips tightening.
He tears her lace
to the rhythm of violins, a piercing note
with piano frozen on an acetate.

They listen, giddy, as she gropes for heaven.
Her invisible hand strokes the microphone.
Still flesh, the three of them break for air,
then spread out their lungs again, ecstatic
like spirits treading the atmosphere.

The Leader

His hand
    has lifted
        and it will give
    the cue again

        this heat-shot afternoon
    outside the arcade
            where the girl
    who stammers pi digits
                on the bus

        grins ten feet behind them
    with tokens spread
    in her palm

        He catches himself
    his hand shot up unknowing
                a gesture that started
        somewhere
on its own

        his fingers poised
    to swat the girl away
or motion
            inward
        for her to join

        He does not love her
but more and more
                his eyes run
    to catch the outliers

the woman with the mad
fluorescent feathers
  who paints portraits
                in minutes
        outside the subway

            the man
          in the wheelchair
      who shouts
          Jesusbewithyou
  and races
      the walkers
    to the curb and back

        Mozart on the headphones
  and Kahlo mustachioed
                by the museum
        so much brilliance
  on this block

  but here on the sidewalk
          the other eyes fix him
          their slow squints pressing
    to keep the tribe
              intact

      Is the greatest achiever
        the one
            who flails alone
  or the one who perfects
            the step in time?

Now his eyes scowl
and he brings his fingers in
　　the girl with a blush trotting
　　　　into their circle

　　　the others staring
　　but parting to make room
　　　　this moment his victory
yes his victory

　　　the power of his voice
　a note deeper than the others
　　　　　his face with stubble
　half a head above theirs

　　　While they shout over joysticks
he slouches in the corner
　　　silent type
　　　　　the one slick enough
　to tilt the day
　　　with his hand.

Elegy for a Rhythm Guitarist

The last thing you hear is a soft chord in A
ringing under the bass at the end of the song,
then a small bit of talk, with the tape running on.
But not in his voice — he had sauntered away.
He muttered, "See you." We nodded our heads.
He slipped out the door, past the bricks and the shed,
and squinted his eyes at the day.

That was five years ago — just a day in July.
He pulled up to the house and slid out of his car
with his clothes all disheveled, but he had his guitar
and he fingered it softly with blanks in his eyes.
In a suburb garage with a tape and some drums,
I sang with Brigitte while he sat down and strummed
a few chords, and the hour passed by.

The story's well-known: how they tracked down his car
smashed apart in a ditch, with his sunglasses snapped
and the packet of joints come apart on his lap.
Ten feet from the window, his broken guitar
which he'd held like a crutch, his eyes red behind shades
through those wandering sessions on long, muggy days —
cigarettes, and the trips to the bar.

A gifted musician; I can't say I knew
him that well, aside from the notes that he played.
Just a friend of a friend; he'd stop by on those days
when the world was stalling. We'd strum a few tunes,
and he'd light up a joint and then blink at the sun

while he hammered the chords, hard and fast, one by one,
as the microphones buzzed in the room.

He had his own troubles: drugged-out and remote,
a high school dropout. A shell of a man
at the end of his life, but he sure had the hands...
And when he blacked out at the side of the road,
the papers that noticed it mentioned his skills,
how he'd taught himself nicely, before he was killed.
(I think I may still have the quote.)

The garage is long gone; I don't live in that town
anymore, though I still sometimes talk to Brigitte
in the house where she still lives, a bit down the street.
The tapes that we made then are lying around
my apartment in piles, except for the one
from that very last session, when we let the tape run,
for I still haven't shaken that sound.

First a roll of the drums. Then the bass wanders in
and the voices flare up, but right there in the back
is the soft chime of strings, and the last artifact —
just a few broken notes, like the drop of a pin
in the balance of time, right before the thread snaps:
when things fall apart, and the last word is trapped
like a ghost in the form of a string.

II

The Activists

He learns to crave her body
reminding himself
that it's impermanent.
He's counted her wounds —
the mark on her shoulder the picket sign left
after months of trudging down the stairs
to the latest demonstration,
the rasp in her voice from shouting at traffic,
the way her throat quivers
when she bolts the food
they bought with the part of their paychecks
they were willing to spare.
Swallowing hunger himself,

he hangs a bag by the carport
and casts his thin arms against it, fearless.
At night, he lies awake with her
on a secondhand mattress, the blinds open,
facing the stars and her poster of Schindler
and listens — never answering —
while she asks
if they would have stood to block the cattle cars.
She tells him love is incitement.
He believes her. Their weekends wind

through cold showers and pipes with the Navajos,
hours awake past midnight on caffeine
with petitions drafted on the table,
her heirlooms, then his
surrendered on the dealer's counter
and turned into cash for the clinics in Sudan.
She leaves for work

and he digs her out of the hamper,
inhales the smell of her
from straps, shirts, her sweatband from jogging.
The early days still haunt him.
Alone in the kitchen,
he replays the First Communion,
high school in the limousine,
the road trips with his grandfather in Texas
when he waved his hand by the window
and pictured empires on the plains.
He holds his eyes steady now,

cool as a sniper, faces down the trucks
that roll looming off the factory farms,
the skyline thick with gas station globes,
savors the hardness of her as she bends
sunburned at the sink in the evening,
the light bulb fading and cans on the stove.
He tells himself, *Nothing but a woman*,
tells himself, *We scavenge together*.

Boy at the Backyard Pond

With a single stone, will you shatter the world?
The reflection holds the same as above —
clouds, sharp branches, the face peering down.

Your muscles hold memory of the ache,
the strain to throw with the grown man's force.
The pain is worth it. What can destroy, can rule.

When you lifted the goldfish bowl above the tiles,
they screamed. Your palms held the fish in place,
the tiny castle, the plastic trees swaying.

A loosing of the grip would splinter the glass.
It is the small worlds the hands can break.
Could the man's knuckles, rising, break the sky?

You set the bowl down then. That was mercy,
their fingers wiping sweat, cries turned to laughter.
Now, the house sleeps. The back door left open

leads to this spot above the reflection:
the windless day, the mirrored fist with gravel
as still and complete as the castle in the bowl.

The first missile flies. For an instant, suspended,
the smaller world holds — the boy and trees
and cloud-coated sky their own frail glass

under the dropping stone. When you dash the surface,
will the sound be worth the silence closing back?
Does the water, finally, swallow every throw?

To Rachanee, Laguna Beach, Jan. 1

Another holidays over and we've asked for less
than we've given away, the alarm's cold chime
waking us to our trusted inventory
of walls, ceiling, slotted sunlight.

To meet the new year, we drive to the streets
where our salaries would never buy a home
and slide six quarters — the year's first price —
into the meter a block from the beach.

Lace fingers, again, and let's enjoy
what is never given to us for keeps:
heaven, the absolute, whatever we name it
mirrored on the surface between wakes and buoys,

the robin's-egg sky that almost dissolves
past the water's edge on bleary days
now bold and separate, presiding master-like
over its more breakable half.

We are one day — always a day, not a year —
closer to broken, our bodies counting
toward an end whose only secret is time and place.
If we are lucky, someday, we will plan our letting go,

but this year is marked for holding what we can.
On the concrete steps, you choose the best angle,
touch your head to mine, click the iPhone camera.
With quarters, we will adore this sky later.

The responsibilities, stored at home, will wait.
How hard do we work to play at pausing time?
We thrive on boundaries pushed just enough,
our bliss bought with coins set aside.

What We're Sure Of

1.

The poet whose grandfather died a week ago hugs me
and presses his card on the dim sum table to assure me
that all orders today are on him. For twenty minutes, longer,
he asks for nothing but stories — his arms folded on the table
and head tilted forward as though attention, rapt focus,
will buy some grace needed for later. My forced punchlines
finally exhausted, he sighs, tearful, and shakes his head.
Everything he knew is gone, he says. We picture memories, jokes,
hard-won lessons slipping away. Earth takes the body
and heaven may admit the soul, but does the mind side
with dust or ascension? Perhaps it floats in the middle,
the leavings of gray matter swirling over tables here
in between scents and steam. *Gone*, for us, may just mean
unreadable, too far for a voice or pen to set in code.
So many others passed today, time and again, and each
freeing of memory may have made the air thicker —
the sun squeezing its way through clusters of particles
and *there* weighing just barely more on each shoulder.
Did creation exist before we learned to imagine it?
How slighter was the world before we gave it names?

2.

Home to prepare for tutoring and I'm relieved that knowledge
is back in its physical bounds: the wooden CD case that I bought
as a child with the discs stacked in chronological order, creased
books on the shelf nearby holding the stories behind each song.
I am glad everything is in its place, but today the spines linger
like unanswered telephones, no incentive to power the speakers
or stretch to reach the top shelf when the gray matter recalls
so much. Even still, I have my old self to thank: the 12-year-old
who raced through homework, thrilled at the blank canvas
of an open hour and bent to listen on repeat to Bob Dylan
sing "A Hard Rain's A-Gonna Fall," each throaty phrase
and connection to the Cold War era adding to the stockpile
of what could someday be cashed in. This week, the U.S.
has mended walls with Cuba. *Fifty years coming*, some say.
The iron curtain looms elsewhere and we still have the tunes for it.
Meanwhile, rain keeps falling — on the road this morning,
I watched a woman huddle with her cart at the bus stop
while a plastic bucket gathered drops beside her. Each cupful
will have its use, laundry or wipes or a boiling mug of tea,
a source to ration; our luck determines what we learn from rain.

3.

At school now and the girl assigned to me laughs, Mark Twain
the white light on her Kindle and even the sober footnotes
close enough to be funny. They call her an English-learner
but that word applies to all of us, the definitions we gather
and pass to others never inventions of our own. She pauses
at *sever*, the cousin of *severe*, and I sketch a flailing hand cleaved
from the arm where it once belonged. *If you sever a hand*, I say,
you have a severe injury. She smiles, tugs a sleeve over her fingers.
Severe, like serious? Like serious, yes, and in no time,
we'll both be serious again — this knowledge we carry a talisman
that does nothing on its own, a ticket merely to buy the food
our stomachs cry for, an incantation against war and the storms
that hammer on our roofs. So many things out to dissolve us!
For what it's worth, we can classify them. The bell rings
and she jots *sever* in her binder, bows on her way to the door.
One more word today, a new prize weightless and hidden,
another piece of the trove assembled a blessing at a time.

Ghost Town Pantoum

In the ghost town, we walk hand in hand,
thin shadows waving over lost saloons
and the ragged posters of medicine shows,
our watches hidden, forgetting time.

Thin shadows waving over lost saloons,
we guess at the names on the faded headstones.
Our watches hidden, forgetting time,
we kiss in the shade of the jail. She tells me

we guess at the names on the faded headstones
as we walk on our own crooked journey;
we kiss in the shade of the jail. She tells me
stories plied from the gospel wagon

as we walk on our own crooked journey.
Her voice is shadow now; the light rays expand.
Stories plied from the gospel wagon
fade on a prayer book's tattered pages.

Her voice is shadow now; the light rays expand
past lovemaking stains on single beds,
fade on a prayer book's tattered pages.
The chapel towers over sunburned land.

Past lovemaking stains on single beds
and the ragged posters of medicine shows,
the chapel towers over sunburned land.
In the ghost town, we walk hand in hand.

Abandoned Shack in Kansas

Something — a hand or the wind or gravity —
  has cracked its defense, set a window board twisting

half a foot toward the highway's spine.
  From the roadside, the car unlocked behind him

and the camera strap heavy on his shoulder,
  the freelancer hovers with his toes against the grass.

A decade ago, at nine, he would have taken
  this invitation, bent the board just far enough

and slid his thin frame into whatever the lock
  protected: explosives, bones, a simple hiding place

washed with silver-gray light. This was
  the domain, the splintered arcade that he

and his friends crept into on the summer days
  together, its only mystique the notion that they

had found it while their rooms had been assigned.
  Once seized, it offered little. A flashlight handy,

they laid out their cards and dice and pushed
  for the coolest spot in the shade, content

in the knowledge that if rules were needed,
  they would make them by decree. Tonight

and tomorrow night, the sanctuaries have
   been named. His father's car will stop at the hotel

for the room his mother booked for him, then roll back
   the next day to the editor's $50 check, the bedroom

that feels less and less his own. It is those promises,
   the odometer and the assigned shots of Dodge

on his camera, that keep him still facing the shack
   and the drying maze of corn. When a car appears,

he runs to fire the engine. The road will collect
   him now. He checks, signals, goes.

One Word

He knows too few words in English
but his title at the top of the page, underlined twice,
points out his favorite: *heaven.*

On the more rickety of the wooden chairs
on the rickety planks of the porch next door,
he sits back-straight in the sun, lets heaven

spill in between the neighbors' jacarandas
and the ice cream truck he urges the kids to chase.
"When I was their age, that was heaven,"

he says, snapping his fingers to the bells,
and his tutor in the better chair, the much younger girl,
gives thumbs-up at the grammar. Their topic is heaven

and his deadline is next Monday, or Tuesday, no rush,
this letter to the local bishop intended
to make his case for confirmation. If heaven

were at stake with this letter, it would take a priest,
not a high school girl, to proof it to perfection,
but he seeks a different sort of heaven

on these three pages stacked to look like one —
these three eased, not torn, from the binder.
The essay, in a word, says: *I deserve heaven,*

or at least it will — the first line still eludes them.
Uncrumpling her own page, the girl suggests
that he make a cluster, write HEAVEN

large in the center and connect the words
that come to mind. All right, then: He twirls his pen
and writes *cars*, *girls*, *Selena*, then quotes: "Thank heaven

for 7-Eleven." They chuckle. "You think that's true?"
he asks, pointing a plumbing-scarred finger
above the trees to what must be heaven

and drawing a jagged line down, past the roofs,
to the market on the corner. "Probably not," he sighs.
With more words, he would say that we've gotten heaven

wrong, that the stars we see are only
the discards, the abandoned ones just bright enough
to evoke with metaphors and headlights, true heaven

a light beyond our corneas, a truth beyond
the words we inscribe. But the unknown is far off now
and today offers its own grace: the makeshift heaven

of a task completed, 500 right words in order
and a neat staple, the seal, in the upper left.
He shrugs, writes the first line: "I want to go to heaven."

The Test

Seeking an initiation
for the skateboard club,
they set their sights on the frazzle-haired man
who sways to headphones on the pool deck
and offers baptism
to the boys who pass alone.

They gather at the minimart,
make plans in a huddle.
If he threatens, five can take him.
No one calls the mission off.
Sweating, they near the pool
and push the tallest one forward,
his low voice speaking for all of them

that they've come to leave sins behind.
With a brown-toothed laugh, the test is on.
The tall one goes first,
his cheeks racing to puff with breath
before the fingers seize and plunge him under.
For a moment, longed for,
the sun dances above

before the surface breaks again
and he chokes, motions help away.
The rest follow, one pushing on the next.
Once home, the jokes finished
about which of them cried or got aroused,

they hurl their clothes in the laundry.
The rest of the afternoon, they abide.
Two comb their Bibles; one cleans, mows the lawn.
A week later, police swarm the complex,
their door knocks and questions
punctuated by news reports

of another attempted baptism on the deck,
a brave girl who kneed the transient and ran.
The two with the Bibles break and confess.
Within an hour, the phone calls begin,
the other three set down by parents and officers
and insisting until the tears burn

that no one was touched below the neck.
Each of them, in another's version,
receives credit for the idea.
The skateboards, confiscated, vanish into lofts.
And the club, with no plans beyond the initiation,
folds by the end of the week.

To the Student Still Without a First Draft Tuesday Morning

If you waste your time, I will waste mine better.
    The weekend's exhausted and here we are again,
        a two-day break usually, but this time it's three —
            I count the days, and, oh, I know

you count them too, your insipid account
    of what you did on Memorial Day weekend
        summed up in three half-giggling words:
            played video games. Yes, I remember those,

and unless my traumatic memories lie,
    they involve plenty of losing: the little spaceship
        exploding, again and again, only to be cued
            back to life by a thumb's distracted tap.

Fingers ready, then! Let's restart the level
    that we did last week. Unless you surprise me —
        and miracles happen; that was the message
            of the poem we read Friday — we will meet

at period's end with your page still empty,
    your seatmate's phone (for I've confiscated yours)
        more gripping than the rights of English women
            during Austen's time. Wednesday, a stunner!

The TV will have stayed off, but your parents
    will have threatened you with lack of dinner
        or something unspeakable if you did homework
            rather than clean your sister's dolls. Thursday,

after I've left two voicemails to discuss
    your grade with your parents — or your sister,
        close enough — you will slump into class,
            your backpack slimmer than usual.

I accidentally threw everything out, you'll say,
    your line from last week — we both loved that.
        If you waste your time, I will waste mine better,
            spend hours up late grading the scraps

you've thought enough to pass forward,
    insist that you haven't crammed the Hemingway
        we both know is inside of you too far deep
            for reclamation. But when I say

that my time-wasting skills trump yours,
    mark my words as more than bragging.
        Rather, consider this: After the long nights
            of youth toiling for the SAT and college,

after the letters and the applications,
    after graduation, grad school and paid-off debt,
        after the handshakes, after the interviews,
            after the credential program and 12-hour days,

after training, taxes, the move, the mortgage,
    a man can blow his time, as I do with you,
        stuck forever on one impassable level,
            and, rather than get calls home for it, get *paid.*

December

I want to be a passenger
in your car again
and shut my eyes
while you sit at the wheel,

awake and assured
in your own private world,
seeing all the lines
on the road ahead,

down a long stretch
of empty highway
without any other
faces in sight.

I want to be a passenger
in your car again
and put my life back
in your hands.

III

Neighborhood

On summer afternoons here, nothing calms
like the red sundown twisted and splayed
through glass in the kitchen, the aged wood door

left open for air and the clang of screen doors
as tag and politics wind down, this street
an open house before the locks go on. Here, even

the gardener slides in like family, pounds the red
dust from his weekday shoes on the mat
and bears his battered cup in, his hair combed to hide

the bald spot and his speech coaxed from memory
about the parched field back home that could
bloom for soccer, yes, bloom for soccer with

just enough topsoil and bleachers for the fans
on afternoons too hot for tag. With care he
slides out the Polaroid of his sister, his sister with

the baby pointing over the field, how parched it is
too hard to tell from the Polaroid but his skin, dry
and cracked, puts *parched* in the air. Can his speech

fail here, in the kitchen, with *parched* in the air
and so much wetness, the tea glasses sweating
and lemons overripe and set to drop on

the tree out front? If lemons can drop and wet
can overflow, then so can coins, spare bills, the last
scraps of allowance that clatter in the bends of the

cardboard cup, too small now to save up
for a car and too small for anything but a parched
smile and *godblessyou*, one more grasp at grace

here in this kitchen with the sun splayed red
through the chandelier, the tea glasses damp and
screen doors clanging, before the locks go on.

Day After New Year's

On the well-behaved days behind the complex gates,
any eyes can volunteer to play police.

This morning, the man in the ironed jacket
appoints himself in charge for a moment,

his slow sidelong gaze at the boys
who loitered too closely to the woman's garage

enough to send them sauntering off.
In an instant, it ends. Walking alone, he passes the girls

who kneel on a blanket beside the new Volvo
and stack their Legos: two boxes, not shared,

the pinks and blues like his sisters once hoarded
in the house on another block years ago.

He stops to watch. One girl glances, sees him,
the pulse that quivers through her face an instant review

of his dark jacket, anonymity, stare.
They leave the Legos in place, duck past the car.

The small one speaks to a shadow through the door.
The man walks on, faster, the neighborhood filled

with the remnants of last week — wreaths left out
for recycling, extensions, unplugged Santas.

The trimmed lawns, the thresholds lay down their rules.
This year will pay the same price for resolution as the last.

The First Thing Mastered

The mornings after the Santa Anas,
his father points him to gather sticks
the wind tore from their tree and the neighbors',
the fence the decider of what is theirs.

The first time, together, they laid out steps.
Grab the fattest part of the wood
and avoid touching the splintered ends.
Walk with them pointed sideways,
never toward the eye.
That first time, he pricked a finger,
went crying for his mother and the Band-Aid.
The second time, not excused,
he set his fingers precisely.

The winds hit every few days this season,
nature's joke on the yard
that barely has time to teeter back.
They clear the grass but seldom walk on it.
The patio holds his mother's reading table,
the deck the tricycle he's outgrown.

To remove sticks is to ask for more.
With every chance, his hands work faster,
fit three or four pieces to a palm
and drop them, bloodless, by the shed.
While his father fires up the mower,
he rewards himself by picking the straightest
and stacking a fort, shoulder-high and trembling,
his own kingdom while the air is still.

Birth

This is
the rush of days in fast forward,
a soundless churn of steam on the kettle,
the sun snared in a mobile making kaleidoscopes on the upstairs wall,
sweat on torn slippers racing up the banister,
the roots of sermons and night confessions piercing through a white
    plastic monitor,
excitement of chatter over morning newspapers with coffee rings
    staining the dictator's face,
steam in clouds hiding Sunday from the mirror,
circle of bloodlines mixed race in the morning pressing frail hands to
    ancestors' fingers,
the moon on the mobile through an alabaster window turning stars
    into mystic ships and tiny men,
invisible telephones ringing unanswered,
the fierce faces of lions and tigers stuffed and tamed on the bedroom
    shelf,
fire trucks on the floor without sirens,
tableau of mother father and child in a crooked living room through
    frayed tree branches,
trinity of soldiers gazing at the dawn burning circles on winter
    driveways,
everyone steadfast too strong to fall.

Grandfather

Through the bedroom door,
left open for the night,
he starts each morning perched
on the edge of the mattress.
Shoulders uneven, skin a crunched paper bag,
he breathes slowly as if waiting
for a cue to stand.

Around the house, his steps are the rituals:
the battered lunch pail filled after breakfast
with the same sandwich, juice and apple.
The glass of scotch poured every evening
to the classical station, in the chair on the right.

The story, the one they whisper,
is that he fled the *People's Army*.
The words explain nothing
but the questions not to ask.
When the house empties, they slide the creaking drawer
to rifle through the unlabeled pictures.
Here in the bent locket, a woman in a wedding dress.
Here a boy and girl by the rice paddy, smiling.

His room becomes the war room,
the hard wood the only floor in the house
flat enough for the soldiers' feet.
The sound echoes here from wall to wall,
the spare white the canvas

for all their dreamed battlegrounds.
He walked in once, knelt,
tapped the plastic Darth Vader.
Real guys like this, he said.
Real guys.

Moment

The girl with the sketchpad
is the lucky one here,

half-drowsy and cooled by handmade fans
in the shade behind the washed-out school,

her throat parched and pencil too tired
to keep its appointment with the page

but beguiled watching the sunken-necked man
in plaid shirt and overalls

who stands at an angle on one leg
and times the skinny boy around the track.

The boy tears around once
and his clothes race to catch him —

the shirt and shorts too big for his frame
billowing behind like sails —

but the blur of his limbs in motion
makes them nearly fill the gaping sleeves.

Passing the man, he breathes loud and staccato
and grins as he picks up speed,

eager as an actor auditioning
to play Prefontaine in the movies.

He will grow taller than the man —
the girl knows, her own brothers the model —

but for now her eyes
ravish both of their shadows,

the boy's sharp like a scythe
cutting brutishly across the corn

and the man's extended, one lanky thumb
hung in his belt loop

while the other taps the stopwatch.
Does he know the splendor

of his form along the grass,
the silhouette that extends from his heels

like a conquered road, a trove of private majesties?
Here, now, the world sighs with him.

It was patience that won here, that set this field green,
this school towering to drink the sun.

When the boy heaves to a stop,
the man hugs him, tousles his hair.

Their arms slung over each other's shoulders,
they blacken the red dirt as they leave,

both of them titans
through a trick of the light.

Four and a Half

I.

The shell is God
and God is in his pocket,
pale blue ridges dotted with sand
that he cups a hand on
running back from the beach.

He hides the shell,
though he knows he did not steal it.
When he knelt over the rocks,
the tide washed it to him,
this small blessing delivered
like a flake of sky.

Ahead, his mother hurries,
one step of hers matching five of his.
If he falls, the shell will shatter.
He locks his fingers, stays upright.

II.

She took him to see God the month before.
In church, he wailed just to wail,
the heads in the rows ahead of him
turning in a ripple, smiling, then back around.

She apologized for him and hoisted him up,
past the pocked stucco walls
and the doorman who made the cross above him.
Outside, red and crying,

she strode to the top of the bluff,
then wrapped her arms tighter, chin by his,
breathing hard as they stared at the blue.
This, she told him, *this is what we can't escape.*

III.

What is heaven like?
he asks them doggedly.
The last answer given never satisfies.

They say heaven is an ocean
without the water,
an air without gravity,
a height above the clouds.

They call it infinity but it is only *higher.*
Does heaven have a ceiling?
Can the ocean roll without its shore?
Even the church, where they bow their heads,
is a house like all the others.

IV.

He has a sister now
and they swathe her in pink.
God's other color, his mother explains —
pink like the roses and the sweet medicine,
her long silk robe,
the blush along her skin.

At its best, at its clearest,
the world codes itself like this:

red for the devil,
the alarms and stop lights;
green for life, the yard after winter.

At the pool, he hears,
a man drowned in the deep end.
Long ago, they repeat. They nudge him toward the blue.
He lowers himself in, the red floater at hand.
The red fingernails coax him closer.
This is safety now, God always hiding,
even in the devil's hue.

Evidence

The runaway's face
still dangles on the light poles,
but if there is a search party,
it has gone indoors today.

From this picture window
on the edge of the palisade,
the city spreads like its own shrugging evidence.

Here, a house, then three more houses
around the loop of a cul-de-sac,
each one positioned
to glance sideways at the others.

She says, *He may have hopped the train,*
then laughs — our only hopping stories
the ones from her grandfather
about ducking the sheriffs,
repeated through cigars, most probably half-true.

It is the city that must have taken the runaway —
this city, or the next across the street,
the unclaimed trails between them
gone with the twentieth-century Westerns.

Still, our comfort is the dream of escape,
the stealing into the territories.

We imagine the house by the highway's edge,
the scarecrow a hundred feet
behind the last thrown newspaper.
We imagine the shaded head in the window
that peeks to see if the crows have gone.

Housewarming, East Los Angeles

Someone across the patio calls the neighborhood *sketchy*
   and the woman at the far end, who has sipped her beer alone
      and tapped her throat to indicate where the operation

took her voice, hoists up a pad and pen and displays them
   like a magician with a handkerchief too thin to pack a dove.
      The few of us between conversations her audience, she starts

with the slim bones of the surroundings: rugged hill above
   the winding street that the parked cars shrink to one lane,
      stray dog slouched on the corner, a single balloon on the rail

that indicates a party at this house up the crooked steps.
   On the patio before the open gate that she sketches without
      the padlock dangling, the crowd half-covers the blank space.

The pen rests for a minute and she shows us our ritual:
   this whiteness marked only by the outlines of gathering,
      the compulsion to touch and not drink alone. Without words

or faces to tell our stories, do the lines show if we celebrate
   or mourn? The new homeowners toast with their margaritas,
      the man's fingers spreading to show the ring to her parents,

but joy and grief make their own congregations — a circle just
   as tight around the landlady who holds her late mother's Polaroid
      and nods eagerly at condolences with her tears having dried.

All that unites us are our neat survivals, this touch of sky
    and nearness with friends what we run to at any hour
        when a room is not enough — the bottles that fizz one by one

an incantation against silence, solitude. Our society captured
    now on her pad, the artist fills in its boundaries. At the curb below
        the steps, three men saunter by and watch, their faces too distant

to read but their gait slowing to signal thirst. Down the block,
    two boys set bottles on the fence and let fly with a slingshot,
        one stone per turn, the game won by what is broken just right.

Awake

When the pinch runner scores, the room can sleep.
Twelfth inning, upstairs, the radio purrs low.
A single clean *crack* will set the night at peace.

This is the sanctuary now — two damp sheets
and a mattress, full moon, water glass overflowed.
When the pinch runner scores, the room can sleep.

Spectral, through dark, the batter pounds his cleats.
Invincible? He must be. The runner inches home.
A single clean *crack* will set the night at peace

and release the hours before. So many things neared
resolution this week: The fingers almost coaxed
Chopin from the keyboard; the eyes fought off sleep

to see the model ship half-built. At moments like these
the world seems set to blossom, a stretch on tip toes
enough to fix the body three inches taller, true peace

a wavering grasp away. Here upstairs, with the stream
of white through drapes, the pennants hang in a row.
When the home team wins, the other fears can sleep.

The pitcher sets now. As the runner takes his lead,
the hands grip a phantom bat, swing, urge the ghost
of the ball into blackness. Just this, and then peace.

When the dreams flow in, there will be no mirrors,
no proof of the callow face, the arms thin as bone.
On that side is perfection. The room must sleep.
If the diamond rests, the diamond rests in peace.

IV

Segue

I.

The first time death comes,
the house freezes and puts up its hands.
What only did its job cannot be blamed:
The soup bowl nourished;
the blankets warmed;
the drapes shaded the eyes at bedside.

II.

Part of the cycle, they say,
but the promise feels broken.
These locks, these rooms they all dust carefully,
should let no one slip away.

III.

At night, the outline still on the mattress,
the boy and girl crouch below it and play detective.
There is no crime here, only a scene.
Can they piece it together?
They share what they know.

Was there a last meal? Yes, the can of soup.
The lips groped for the hot, steady spoon.
Was there a last song? Yes, the old Sinatra
on the turntable, slapped there in haste.
Were there last words? Yes. The mother heard them
whispered in her ear, but will not say.

IV.

They open the drapes
to let the sun spill back.
The light changes what none of them will.
The grandfather's cigarette
waits mashed in the tray,
craved when it was inhaled last.
His solitaire hand, almost won,
waits for the few face-down cards.

V.

Were there second to last words? Third? Fourth?
Not knowing the answer, they hug and cry.

VI.

The morning of the funeral,
they invent new orders.
Breakfast starts at seven sharp,
coats and ties on around the table.
Mourning will cost $1.50 —
the tollbooth fee. Each one offers quarters.
The boy helps the girl into the car,
shuts her door for the first and last time.

Singer on River Street, Savannah, Georgia

With a few words, did you place her in the front row?
Her eyes, raw from elsewhere, beg your attention.
Perched apart from the rest, she is the hungriest one.

Did she come to see you? Your mind traces back
the last week's sequence — first your text to the drummer
that he passed to the agent, the agent to the booking man,

the booking man's tip that set the newspaper rolling.
The front page displayed you. Whooping, you drank till dawn.
On the quiet nights, awake in your dorm room,

you stare at the sky and dream its machinery.
How many gears does it hold? Can your words conduct them?
Through so many reactions, you took the stage

in this city kept by chance, the blocks that Sherman spared
the backdrop as you tuned and set the tip jar down.
In this room may be connections, the unexpected prize

that the right song or smile brings. The woman watches you
watch her. She swallows, cups her hands for warmth.
You say she sought you, not shelter, that her wet feet wound

past the tall ship, the carriages, the rain-spangled river;
the current you started with your fingers on the pad
has changed the motion of the street here, placed a body

where no body was before. Where does the current
go from here? Does she stay? Depart by dawn?
Everything offstage suspended, you cue the next song.

Their Mother and the Coyote

The trap pounced onto its foot
from the patch of hay behind the rose bushes,
she sprints inside to call Animal Control
then slowly creeps out, as gingerly

as chancing the river's surges.
The man who set the trap for them
away at work with the car and rifle,
every step she takes refines the rules —

when she freezes, the children freeze,
then waver behind her in single file.
In the jaws, half-white and lurching, is the catch.
The wild eyes them and they eye it back,

their uneasy laughter the triumph now
against its outraged oval mouth,
its front legs that shrink and bound up straight
as if trying to cow the roof behind them.

Is this the one that devoured the dogs
around the block? The boy darts in
and comes back with the cap gun, aims it,
but his mother faces the animal with only

her hands spread out, the thorn-pocked palms
survivors of the yard's lesser battles.
This dirt is theirs and for the moments
before the engine roars up, so is the coyote.

From an arm's length, cinched in its trap,
it struts and dazzles. What is tempered already
shrinks back. They live in this pulsing
space between, these few invincible feet.

Park in Reykjavik, Iceland

The wind
        has snatched the Frisbee
                and the boy

    scrambles into the bushes
            to catch it in flight

as though the ground
        would score a point
                for touching it first.

In shorts, he slackens
        and bolts back straight

    to navigate the branches
           that cut him already.
                When he throws

the Frisbee to the woman
        who left her purse half-spilled

on the bench,
        the wind deflects it
           and cues the race again.

    No one reads
        the newspaper that dances
              across the square

by the flower garden,
        but there must be news

           about wind somewhere:

a typhoon that tore roofs

                off the huts in Ghana

or a man who died of chill

              in the coldest capital.

So often the elements

          give us hints

                  of what they're capable of;

if we stay whole

        through them,

              we call it bravery, sport.

Today at the Blue Lagoon,

             I watched two men wince

at the jagged rocks

        under the steaming surface

but walk until the heat

        nearly blistered

before the signs by the incline

           that urged *No Entry*.

The edges too blunt

       to puncture skin

            cause the feet not to turn

but to step on boldly,

       and sometimes even blood —

a scar to keep —
                only tempts us
                        to laugh off more.

  At the park now, the boy
                  rolls his pant leg higher

to show his mark
                to the younger one beside him,
                              this red jag

  that will heal to pink
                the new trophy.
                    The woman

   shakes her purse,
            shakes her head,
                  no tissue in sight.

The wind,
          which started this,
                will fan the leg dry.

Our Money's Worth

Saturday at the Honda dealer,
two more errands to go,
we park it for the last time
and wet a tissue to rub the stain
from the frayed plastic top of the key.

In a bright, hot office,
we smile wanly at the numbers:
200,000 miles without a breakdown
worth $1,500 when traded in.
As the woman explains the spreadsheet
(no bargain in the offing),

the frail man through the glass door
widens an eye to meet the headlamp
he steadies his thin rag to shine.
In our thirties now,
we have logged enough milestones
to know not to dwell on new ones,

and so when the woman sighs
Two hundred thousand without a breakdown,
we nod that, yes, the dealers served it well —
snow tires in Connecticut
and lubes on the desert drives,
no seam on the side mirror from the shop
after the hit-and-run at the curb.

A signature now, two hard handshakes
and we toast with bottled water
to what did not let us down —
no Jim or Luke or Pedro
here in factory clothes to thank in person,
luck the only name we can give
to what kept each wheel steady,
the brakes resilient and tight.

Last Date Before the Proposal

This is the quiet negotiation,
the laying of terms, the unspoken drawing
of the boundary between two sides
that will be reached across but never breached.

The ritual starts at a sunlit table.
Each of us has been here before.
There is nothing to sign,
nothing to bring but intentions.
The past has taught us what to keep in sight.

Over untouched teas, we discuss Kurosawa.
You call him a humanist. I have forgotten his films.
It is not about them
but the way you say *humanist*.
We are auditioning parts. If this voice softens,

it may be the one to stir awake
and rasp comforts at two in the morning.
And look at this hand — it is scarred from tools,
but trembles to hold the wine glass steady.
This hand will not rage. We know all the scenes

to come, the leases signed in confidence
and the shoulders stroked over doctor's papers,
the path that reverses in time
to these two parking spots, this corner of the diner.
The road begins when we end suspicions.
We part with a handshake, disguised as a kiss.

January

(I know) I'm losing you
we speak
the words in parentheses
never raising our voices enough
to rattle the ice
on the locked windows
a newspaper lies
with its secrets open
around the plates on the kitchen table
the last stains of yesterday's meals
left drying
in sunbeams
your sweat still clings
to the aging mattress
the nights that we lie awake together
your breaths thin
arms aromatic
with the hot musk of secondhand coats
sometimes I watch you
(you must know this)
naked inside the morning mirror
chest hanging casually
eyes tracking patterns
in the gray hair swirling
between your fingers
(I remember the sweat lines
the stifled laughs
shivering up the stairs in winter

two waists entwined on a couch
red-eyed
the floor scattered with a younger man's shoes)
we live
in solitudes
smile across them
pack universes in our drawers
wake at dawn
to the roar of engines
pounding a new day
through the rush of snow
only
those moments in the evening
when the sky pulls low
you lean against me
wrap your fingers
around the hands
that brushed the makeup off your cheeks
murmur the words
you heard last night
in dreams about ascending
(lights blinding
I know)

Ride Home

His mother's eyes without a mouth in the mirror,
he slouches, rain-drenched, loose like a doll.

The one prize from the fair, the stuffed red giraffe
that she shelled out to help him win, curls in his arm.

This outing was their secret, her red circle made
on the calendar this morning, a day marked for nothing else.

To break the silence after each wipe on the windshield,
she asks him to name his favorite part.

The ball toss, he mutters, his focus on the window.
He picks a hair off his crown, scowls, sets it back.

The ball toss will do. A favorite of any kind leaves
the day won, resolved, a label stuck on what is clear.

At home, they will ease back into the put-off questions,
the studied tact, three asleep in different rooms.

The man will take the giraffe's picture. The heater will start,
their shoes kicked off in a heap to dry together.

Over soup, they will say grace for what is second-rate —
thanks, like secrets, the art of leaving the right parts unsaid.

The Ones Who Disappeared

In the meetings with old friends, rarer each year,
they shrink to their mannerisms. Conjured in asides,
they become the limp and the saved candy wrappers,

the closed guitar case and the tattered biography
leafed through each morning at the back of the gym.
Once gone, they gave way. The hands that cleared June

off the scrap paper tables threw out the class work;
new strangers claimed the desks, a fresh coat of paint
any last graffiti. From the first two yearbooks,

they stare like the rest, pinned and unfinished
against the gray-white screen. It is the dreams
that force them to walk in color,

that stretch their images countlessfold
and probe until dawn for what the grains reveal.
Does this squinted eye see something out of frame?

A beckoning smile? A chance at shelter, love?
Was the road they escaped on bolder and brighter,
a better deal than for those who stayed?

Ofrenda for John Gardiner

1947-2017

When we met, you were thirty-two steps ahead of me
on the hill that only slopes one way, those gone before you

having tossed their words, their madnesses down
onto your shoulders as you carried them higher —

the workshop founded in the 1960s and so many
conversations about Kerouac and codeine

now forgotten by so many, your randy tiger of a voice
booming them awake again for the younger poets

Saturday afternoons at the library, your yellowed
pulp magazines providing epigraphs as you whittled

rants about Bush, poachers, the Internet — all of us
half-polite in the children's space. Dear clown,

teacher, jester who sweetened so much anger, I dreamed
last night that we all hoisted your own words and trudged

up that hill ourselves, the top uncertain but our burning still
to let nothing drop below us. Up those cliffs, those smashed

coyote drags that turned celestial in your poems,
we left the drivers below who buzzed over crosswalks

and let Laguna stay beautiful and crippled as you knew it —
even the drivers, now that we realized, fragile enough

to be someone's brothers. We shouldered your words
because they can only rest on shoulders now, your voice

too far gone to call them back for revision. They will spin
in place if the stars' axles will hold them. We should take this,

I suppose, as our blessing, the gnarled cliffs that point
up instead of down — the angle tilting our chins toward

what is higher, toward where wonder begins when we've
exhausted sand and sediment, all our best maybe in sight.

V

Commencement Day

The email, a last leap for glory,
  calls for 117 of them
    to meet to pray at sunrise
      at the lake by Humanities Hall,

the two sawed-off trunks
  and the rowboat overturned ashore
    the seating for the earliest risers.
      Only three show up: the RA first

with his psalm book, staking out
  one trunk, the surfer in torn jeans
    and his twin sister parking
      half-awake on the dirt and rubbing

back sleep. The RA almost shouts
  to hear his voice skim the water,
    but smiles, combs the hair
      he slicked carefully in the mirror

and without speaking, calls off
  the prayer. His name on the email
    that went mostly untouched,
      he follows the flashes across

the top of the lake and knows,
  one more time, that stillness is right —
    that the campus has slipped
      beyond the urging of his words

and fingers, the other 115
  now in the havens of separate rooms,
    the morning with no plans but picked-at
      brunches and private jubilations.

Sighing, beaming, he extends his arms
  before the lake and lets the wind
    rush through. The twins shrug
      and toss their Bible in the truck

but linger, the glinting sun
  and water still promising something —
    some ecstasy or transformation,
      some chunk of grace stolen

from this hazy morning they set
  their alarms to see. They find it
    in the rowboat, its bent spine
      that juts up toward the sky

like a muscle flexed defiantly
  through the smashed paint and rust.
    From her pocket, the sister
      draws a single silver marker.

Her brother's turn is first.
  Passing the pen back and forth,
    they scrawl their names and birthdate,
      then spatter the hull with the record

of their imagined last four years:
  the red-eye flights they passed on
    now taken for posterity, the offices
      not run for now chased and won,

this very lake ravished day
  after day each season, the eyes
    missing study for the swells at dawn.
      With a coffee cup's tap, they bless

the boat. Their still-waking muscles
  turn it over and push. Through the water,
    it cuts a sharp, steady path, the surface
      closing behind it, erasing the seam.

Desert Highway, New Year's Eve

A quiet brush of the apocalypse,
a splash of orange behind the low clouds
bathes her skin as she steps down the canyon,
echoes muffled underneath her soles.

A sandstorm is coming and the desert waits
to grow tighter in the bleeding dusk,
the short trees to bend, invisible currents
to churn dust from the mouths of craters.

He sits on the ledge, too distant to hear her,
her coat in his lap. The chrome of their wheels
rusts to brown in the canceling shadows,
the tire treads scratching a wavering road.

He swallows, rubs the sweat on her collar
as she sinks away from him down the valley,
watches the muscles flex in her shoulders
and push back the cold. *I just need a walk,*

she whispered to him. *Can you stay behind
and guard the camper?* She stretches now,
displays the arms that carried her luggage
when they took to the motels in August,

the legs that hardened standing in line
for pills, bail bonds, loans. As she bends
to tear a rose from the brush, he feels
his tattoos burn again, mouths the words

he tried that morning when she stood at the window
and dreamed out loud about a silent world
without alarms or sirens, the men deserted
from the bars she worked in every other city,

her car disappearing in a white garage
on a street of houses blending together,
a picket fence and a lawn. She ascends
the valley again, slides her own door open,

wraps the coat back around her shoulders.
They drive and the clouds sink lower. That night,
as she lies face down on motel pillows,
he pictures her walking alone again

through the desert, the only figure left moving
in a shattered landscape of brush and bone
as if God had set creation backward,
let the footsteps perish one at a time

and left her to explore, her arms
relaxed at last in the arid evening,
her skirt gliding around unfinished roots
and coyotes fallen in ravines. Like a child,

she slides off her shoes, extends a finger
to brush the inescapable veins
of a perfect leaf, the infinite patterns
of snakeskin impaled on a jagged stone,

then dances, weightless, across the canyon,
her fists high, spinning in orange glow
as the world lies back and waits to pass under
when the last pair of eyes is closed.

The Pool Coach Sings Hallelujah

Only during the solo drives
does he marvel at the things done correctly.
At 5 each morning, sparked by caffeine
and perched in uniform behind the wheel,
he cues the gospel station
and cruises through the sleeping city,

Aretha and the Nightingales
overpowering his reedy tenor
as the shapes of buildings rise
under the sprawl of constellations.
Here, nothing shows but the majesties:
the steeple that juts
to meet the purple-black dawn,

the refinery towers
that the plaque on the library
says built this county out of dirt and grime.
With sunrise come the imperfections.
The sophomore is pregnant again,
the candles from the last drive-by
melted by the porch a mile from campus.
In his dreams, some nights,

he watches the coach's outlines
saunter without him around the pool —
the staccato hand against the clipboard
turning temper into music,
the legs ambling, then snapping to strides
to keep the boys at attention.

He is the placeholder this fall,
shorter than the one from spring;
his voice is too high, his shoulders low.
But at freshman practice,
he spots the hungry looks,

the trust in him the quiet ones
beam sideways across the deck.
Between the swears and towel snaps,
they seek his assurance, his veteran's guile.
They plead to know how to harness precision,
to tame the water and rise.

Young Father

The house still undone
from his bark and the slammed front door,
he ponders a jacket, then faces the yard
in tank top and paint-smeared jeans.
The neighbors' girl in the wading pool
stares as his mind sizes up his person:
the stubble on his chin,
good for scaring coyotes.
The dirty jeans, a sign of work.

The door will survive
just as it toughed the last earthquake.
No carpenter, he scans the homes down the block
and pretends to figure out the supports.
Behind the pastel walls,
the boards clench in some machinery,
some intricate weights and balances
to quell the unexpected blows.

Before long, his mind will reshuffle the story:
He shouted first, or maybe the boy,
something interjected about toys in the kitchen
or a forgotten promise of a ride.
The woman kept quiet, pressed the boy to her stomach.
She holds the foundation, stills the pulses
that the walls tuck, wavering, inside.
They do their best here, the ones who moved in
after someone else conquered the wild.

Professor

Her office hours,
after her eightieth birthday,
moved to a bench
overlooking the shore,
she goes without *hello*
when the students hover by her.
It is the birds' arrival
that invites her grin,
the buck teeth and gum scar
she has given up concealing.
The questions on the reading
answered only with questions,

the students cap their pens
and watch the tide shatter, roll.
I am giving myself back, she says.
Her toes stretch to meet the water.
This year, she parted with the car,
gave her late husband's things
to the Good Will finally.
If only one student shows,
she calls a walk along the harbor.
The conversation leaves Plato
and moves on to sea levels,

the moorings and safety signs
that the water will cradle
inch by inch.
Does every triumph
lead to this spot:

this overcast beach
with food for the gulls,
the eyes that squint
through stray hairs

to watch the motorboats fade?
I am giving myself back, she says again.
Her fingers slow enough
to keep the shakes at bay,
she spreads the Ziploc bag
and holds the crumbs
before tossing them.
Each one flies like a considered gift,
a bargain for what the next world
may repay.

Crossing, Harpers Ferry

Ten minutes since the gas station and the map is lost already,
    let loose for an instant by distracted fingers and swept
        by the breeze across shoe tops half a block down.

To make our maps was achievement, centuries of fine hands
    setting the lines in place before the cameras proved
        what we had guessed correctly, but with

the rivers so close, it is as good a time as any to surrender
    the markings that pointed us here. In the skeleton
        of this Civil War town where caretakers

work to preserve the bones, we celebrate the age of what
    can be traced to a year: John Brown's fort marked
        with a mounted placard while the gift shops

declare that uprisings here are through. Today's sightseeing
    begins in the town, but the road consummates in what
        thrills beyond it: two metal railings that intersect

as the Shenandoah and Potomac rage together. What we find
    charming past this point is up to us, the harsh churn
        of mud and branches, day and night, marking

the side where might has its way. Do we defeat the current only
    by staying out of its path? Up the hill, the aged hotels
        sit above overflow's reach, while the foot bridges

lure us on trips that borderlines proclaim. On this bank, our feet
    touch West Virginia; a walk across, an ease off the handrail,
        and we gaze back from Maryland. Even when

the water separates them for us, we know the states count
         for something — years of construction and Constitution
                  firming the feats we call our own. This town

stands, ready for evening, benches poised toward the river. For $1
         at the gift shop, a map offers the safe routes back, our
                  settlements the stops between what can only flow.

Museum of Tolerance

The shirtless man by the ticket counter
　　has already broken the gloom here, his crowd
　　　　of two boys and the cashier with the Star of David
　　　　　　gathered around and mouthing astonishment

as he tells the tale behind every scar.
　　Yes, this one on the side was from the camp —
　　　　he tells them not to be shy to ask —
　　　　　　when he tripped into the ditch

on the run after stealing cigarettes,
　　the one on the knuckle from punching the soldier
　　　　in the bar, brave with whiskey, a decade after.
　　　　　　Touch it, he snarls, jutting out his fist.

That split a real Nazi's lip.
　　In the rooms behind him, the voices lay low
　　　　but touch is the rule, the extended families
　　　　　　passing in fours and fives as tight

as at church or the carnival. Are they
　　all survivors here, dazed and exhilarated
　　　　by the fate that dropped them so far from blight?
　　　　　　A father heads the line, shirt fat with muscles

and a single proud thumb pushing the stroller;
　　the woman and girl hug sideways, then again,
　　　　tight as dancers in a row. At each display,
　　　　　　the time lines and the whispered assurances

reiterate that what is done is done.
   Pol Pot is dead, the children of Kampuchea
      reading again to go to college; Rwanda
         has forgiven itself and opened supermarkets;

the ghettos are demolished, the Cold War won.
   Sudan, they skip. For now, the beasts are gone.
      They face the new life, the one after the mending,
         after the last mistakes were made.

Bonfire at Cape Cod with Marge Piercy's Workshop

No one has brought a first draft. On this smooth strip of beach
that someone pocked with a shovel, two feet deep and wide,

we use the ordinary items for kindling: the same front page
of the *Cape Cod Times* wadded again and again to fit

the gaps between logs, thin planks with nails still stuck out
and curled. When the last embers burn out, only the nails

will keep their shape — our materials outlived by what almost
held them together. For the last week around the table,

we've dissected our scraps. The words worth keeping
have gone to folders and the rest to piles, compost or recycling,

whatever fate we assign to our thoughts that will not survive
the year. The useful things will still serve us. The binders

that held our worst drafts will hold our best someday,
the pens retain their ink, the tide continue to crash

even if all we can write is that it crashes a lot, loudly,
a rhythm we read too much into. Here on the sand,

the work week done, we are content to watch the show.
The flames toss up patterns, flash, then withdraw them;

the sky pulls its nightly trick, wrings red and pink from blue.
When it darkens, we head back. With our directions,

in separate cars, we navigate the roads without names,
finesse the sharp turns, one hand ready on the brights

until we return to the cabins, the locked doors and luggage,
our retreat to the things we know better than to lose.

Alaska Airlines Nonstop to LAX

Before the planes turned to ram the Twin Towers,
they hummed in a straight line just like this —
an achievement always to stay calm facing forward
and most remarkable when wings and circuits
keep us suspended over a space too vast
to be even called a drop. The sky that radiates blue
from below turns to nothing when looked at
from above, but here on board, we cling
to the somethings we have: water closer to us
in the plastic bottles than in the particles
of clouds, *American Hustle* on the in-flight movie
catching more stares than the mountaintops
that will never bounce light just this way again.
The story goes that even the astronauts
played Hank Williams on Apollo 13
until the batteries died, and perhaps in the face
of the possible fireball, all we know is the language
we packed from home. Given one more minute,
how many of us would opt for last words,
some grand phrase to resolve up high
what was left unfinished miles below?
The fullest circle would be to go in silence,
to let sky outlive the word for sky
and thrill one last time to what light and color gave —
the outpost of ground and expansion of blue
and the promise that thoughts could help us climb.

Blues Man

One century (which time let go)
lives on stubbornly in this room.
The speakers hum with tales
of Sunday gospel, police dogs on the shoals,
bootleg whiskey at the back of a bus
in Chicago after the war.
Thirty chairs and a light turned low
give shelter from the cold outside
where the word 'legend' is scrawled in black
by the photograph on the window.
Hoarse, white-haired, he squints at the figures
who watch him back from the crooked tables,
his fingers conjuring the notes from childhood,
his foot on the case tapping rhymes.

You're healed now, say the thin girl's eyes.
I'm out of change, says the man with the jar.
A couple sways in the dark by the counter;
the boys sit up front, eager, taking notes down.

Their pens sustain him. At ten, alone,
he walks by the ghosts of a college town,
the bootleggers painted solemn on
the gallery walls, Chicago beamed
into the multiplex, the gnash of police dogs
pantomimed through a flickering reel,
the bus stopping by the curb to take him
to his next one-night stand, the headlights gold
as the waitress shuts out the light,
unscarred,
and heads for the dead of home.

Acknowledgements

Grateful acknowledgement is made to the editors of the following publications in which these poems first appeared:

American Mustard: "The Chicago Window Washer Lets His Soap Paintings Stay"

Angels in Seven (Moon Tide Press, 2016): "Poems at the Station," "To Rachanee, Laguna Beach, Jan. 1," "What We're Sure Of," "To the Student Still Without a First Draft Tuesday Morning," "Our Money's Worth," "Ride Home," "Alaska Airlines Nonstop to LAX"

Cadence Collective: "Woman Next Door," "One Word," "Day After New Year's"

College Town (Tebot Bach, 2010): "Soprano," "The Activists," "Ghost Town Pantoum," "Birth," "January," "Desert Highway, New Year's Eve"

Faultline: "Elegy for a Rhythm Guitarist"

The First Thing Mastered (Tebot Bach, 2013): "Newborn," "The Leader," "Boy at the Backyard Pond," "Abandoned Shack in Kansas," "The Test," "The First Thing Mastered," "Grandfather," "Moment," "Four and a Half," "Evidence," "Awake," "Segue," "Singer on River Street, Savannah, Georgia," "Their Mother and the Coyote," "Last Date Before the Proposal," "The Ones Who Disappeared," "Young Father," "Professor"

Golden Streetcar: "Ofrenda for John Gardiner"

Lummox: "Museum of Tolerance"

Muddy River Poetry Review: "Housewarming, East Los Angeles"

Pea River Journal: "Neighborhood"

Poetry Quarterly: "The Beatles at 80," "Bonfire at Cape Cod with Marge Piercy's Workshop"

Potomac Review: "Crossing, Harpers Ferry"
Rockhurst Review: "Commencement Day"
Sage Trail: "College Town"
San Pedro River Review: "The Pool Coach Sings Hallelujah"
Thief After Dark (FarStarFire Press, 2002): "Host," "December"
Tide Pools: An Anthology of Orange County Poetry (Moon Tide Press, 2006): "Blues Man"
Zocalo Public Square: "Park in Reykjavik, Iceland"

Thanks, in no particular order, to Eric Morago, Susan Davis, Carole Luther, Mifanwy Kaiser, Marge Piercy, Lee Mallory, Ricki Mandeville, Kate Buckley, Mike Sprake, Anna Marie Dunlap, Catherine Spear, Annette Schlichter, Jane Hilary, Gabriella Miotto, Sue Cross, James Ysidro, Carrie Pohlhammer, Angela Apodaca, Loraine Ferrara, Zoot Velasco, Stephanie Brown, Casey Newton, Marjie Blevins, MaryAnn Easley, G. Murray Thomas, John Perry, Thomas R. Thomas, Myrenna Ogbu, Marrie Stone, John and Ann Brantingham, Jeff and Tobi Alfier, Ben Trigg, Steve Ramirez, Jaimes Palacio, Tamara Trujillo, Roger Perez, Irena Praitis, S.A. Griffin, Mindy Nettifee, Carine Topal, Michael Ubaldini, Gail Newman, Michael Kramer, Peggy Dobreer, Timothy Matthew Perez, Sharon Venezio, Robbi Nester, Ruth Bavetta, Paul Kareem Tayyar, Brendan Constantine, Elena Karina Byrne, David St. John and Grant Hier — plus the Poetry Foundation, the Academy of American Poets, the Muckenthaler Cultural Center, and the most loving and supportive family I could ever ask for.

This book is dedicated to the memory of Peter Srisavasdi, Amanda Walzer and John Gardiner — "Their bodies are buried in peace, but their name liveth for evermore."

About the Author

Michael Miller is a former entertainment journalist for the *Los Angeles Times* and the author of *Thief After Dark* (FarStarFire Press, 2002), *College Town* (Tebot Bach, 2010), *The First Thing Mastered* (Tebot Bach, 2013) and *Angels in Seven* (Moon Tide Press, 2016). A two-time Pushcart Prize nominee, he won a 2014 Orange County Press Club award for his story on poets Lee Mallory and Charles Bukowski. He earned a BA in English from UC Irvine and an MA in creative writing from the University of East Anglia. He currently lives in Los Angeles with his wife, Rachanee Srisavasdi, and their daughter, Clare.

Patrons

Moon Tide Press would like to thank the following people for their support in helping publish the finest poetry from the Southern California region. To sign up as a patron, visit www.moontidepress.com or send an email to publisher@moontidepress.com.

Anonymous
Robin Axworthy
Conner Brenner
Bill Cushing
Susan Davis
Peggy Dobreer
Dennis Gowans
Alexis Rhone Fancher
Half Off Books & Brad T. Cox
Jim & Vicky Hoggatt
Ron Koertge & Bianca Richards
Ray & Christi Lacoste
Zachary & Tammy Locklin
Lincoln McElwee
David McIntire
José Enrique Medina
Andrew November
Michael Miller & Rachanee Srisavasdi
Terri Niccum
Ronny & Richard Morago
Jennifer Smith
Ben Trigg
Andrew Turner
Mariano Zaro

Also Available from Moon Tide Press

At the Table of the Unknown, Alexandra Umlas (2019)
The Book of Rabbits, Vince Trimboli (2019)
Everything I Write Is a Love Song to the World, David McIntire (2019)
Letters to the Leader, HanaLena Fennel (2019)
Darwin's Garden, Lee Rossi (2019)
Dark Ink: A Poetry Anthology Inspired by Horror (2018)
Drop and Dazzle, Peggy Dobreer (2018)
Junkie Wife, Alexis Rhone Fancher (2018)
The Moon, My Lover, My Mother, & the Dog, Daniel McGinn (2018)
Lullaby of Teeth: An Anthology of Southern California Poetry (2017)
Angels in Seven, Michael Miller (2016)
A Likely Story, Robbi Nester (2014)
Embers on the Stairs, Ruth Bavetta (2014)
The Green of Sunset, John Brantingham (2013)
The Savagery of Bone, Timothy Matthew Perez (2013)
The Silence of Doorways, Sharon Venezio (2013)
Cosmos: An Anthology of Southern California Poetry (2012)
Straws and Shadows, Irena Praitis (2012)
In the Lake of Your Bones, Peggy Dobreer (2012)
I Was Building Up to Something, Susan Davis (2011)
Hopeless Cases, Michael Kramer (2011)
One World, Gail Newman (2011)
What We Ache For, Eric Morago (2010)
Now and Then, Lee Mallory (2009)
Pop Art: An Anthology of Southern California Poetry (2009)
In the Heaven of Never Before, Carine Topal (2008)
A Wild Region, Kate Buckley (2008)
Carving in Bone: An Anthology of Orange County Poetry (2007)
Kindness from a Dark God, Ben Trigg (2007)
A Thin Strand of Lights, Ricki Mandeville (2006)
Sleepyhead Assassins, Mindy Nettifee (2006)
Tide Pools: An Anthology of Orange County Poetry (2006)
Lost American Nights: Lyrics & Poems, Michael Ubaldini (2006)

www.ingramcontent.com/pod-product-compliance
Lightning Source LLC
Chambersburg PA
CBHW020915090426
42736CB00008B/641